Missing Persons Report

Accounts from the Mushroom Cloud

poems by

A. C. Dreher

Finishing Line Press
Georgetown, Kentucky

Missing Persons Report

Accounts from the Mushroom Cloud

ACKNOWLEDGMENTS

Thank you to Shannon, "Doc," Leslie, Jill, Ruthie, Laura, Phil, Josh, Jason, Jack,
Vaughn, and Mitchell. Suffice it to say that without each of you, this would not
have been.

Publisher: Leah Maines

Editor: Christen Kincaid

Cover Art: A.C. Dreher

Author Photo: Jack Cantey

Cover Design: Elizabeth Maines McCleavy

Printed in the USA on acid-free paper.
Order online: www.finishinglinepress.com
also available on amazon.com

Author inquiries and mail orders:
Finishing Line Press
P. O. Box 1626
Georgetown, Kentucky 40324
U. S. A.

Table of Contents

To my family, especially Mom and Dad, thank you for always supporting my writing.

Southpaw by Way of Apology

I.

when stalactites formed ice tornadoes we slept
my ear to your chest   our legs braided
wrapped in furs like a chrysalis
and tagged "do not open until"

spring came and sun-dappled the cave mouth
you were so excited you danced
arms full of purple lupine
you pulled my hair and bit my lip

I trusted my bone strength to organ meat then
those dark months my eyes never adjusted
when you nearly forgot yourself as a polar bear
you doubled over suddenly grew crescent-toothed   white-haired

before I could suffer the long ice-float death
you took my arm   or meant to   but sharp claws
pierced gentle veins   and ever since I bled
out over the permafrost you've tried to restore balance

II.

in a future iteration
you ate electricity like Edison's elephant
and became southpaw by way of apology

you forgot yanking me from the river
pushing water from my coughs
you forgot scars on my chest
were never your doing

III.

you were there when Emperor Qin burned tomes
rounded up philosophers and poets
I watched
you into the pit with the rest
soldiers picked up shovels
I felt dirt on my forehead
a boot on my back

smart students   we took the lesson
suppression our price for unity
so we've watched across rivers and meridians

I must have ended it once
when we'd seen too many terra-cotta armies
and we'd never make the border
without false papers
your palm pressed warm on the back of my neck
when you kissed me goodbye

IV.

you must have ended it once
on a blanketed pickup truck bed
        who knew where that could go?
staring at a farmhouse and autumn leaves
giving way to winter constellations
nowhere good   you thought
mid-sip two malts in
you ran for the treeline
for a year I thought you'd frozen to death

but I am happy you kindled love and survived
so I've never told details
of my train wreck rebirth
that I died young and came back
with ribs that still ache when it rains

since then I've been imprinted with your shadows
not the ephemera   not your favorite ice cream
but your stormcloud eyes
your tendency to muss your hair
how the roar quiets when you focus
a heart more sensitive than delicate instruments
you use to explain behaviors of light

V.

we orbit like prizefighters
eager for rematch
I hear the drum too   you know
I tell you   nowhere good is what I'm used to
and your lips press into a line

before you part them to drink Plato's river
and forget everything
before I crash-land this Plane of Oblivion
please stall   ask Odysseus how
I'm flying without a helmet   my hair full of purple flowers

Postcard from California

I read our future in candy wrappers,
but I accidentally threw them away afterward and, well,
I've slept since then. We'll never know what could
have been if you had kept writing after you sent that postcard
from California. The one with the chaotic art that
reminded me of standing in front of Chagall's windows, arms out, and
spinning like a helicopter till the blue glass and my propeller blurred.

The trick is to focus on something else—baseball,
like anything, is a game of attention. I'm calling
for pitches but the guy on the mound keeps shaking his head.
The audience sighs and I rub some dirt into my glove.
I thought he was cute till I saw him spit tobacco juice,
but it turned out to be just a peanut shell or postage stamp.

When the Cubs lose, my friend doesn't talk to me for days
but I don't know how far this goes and who all is involved.
Once I awoke lying in front of the Chagall windows
holding a catcher's mask. The medic said I could run home
if I wanted—I was hoping your postcard would still be safe
under the mattress. The thing about adulthood is
no one checks my candy for poison anymore.

33 Percent

Nearly all I can remember is aftermath:
a door out of line with its frame
that will never close, a nervous twitch,
a loose thread that once pulled
undoes an entire seam. The fingernail
picks the scab, and new blood seeps.
I leave *or* for those higher up the food chain.

My mouth is full of lies and secrets in a language I cannot speak,
compressed into a cube I cannot digest.
Its corner pokes my optic nerve sometimes.
But I've numbed the root of my tongue so I can't taste bitterness
or gag on burning betrayal with no chaser.
V i c t. There is mathematically no more than 33-percent difference.
A tongue depressor scrapes smooth, pink scar tissue.

For this my mind sews labyrinths and plants tricks;
this... *I*... *m*... cannot seem to see it—say it
plainly, the code I do not break,
for many, many years of dreams, unraveling,
unearthing tent stakes I had hammered down.
This, why the withered trust, reluctant handshake or hold,
the rise of anger like bile.

Nearly all I can remember is aftermath.
If I could arrange an accounting of the mushroom cloud
the damage seems infinite.
I have never known a world without fallout,
without soil turned to acid underfoot,
without the deceit of viscous fluids when blood can be thinned
to nothing, to wine, or scattered to trillions of atoms...
This, why I climb walls obliquely, every step with bent toes
a reclamation of history.

Komposita: A Dream

You said blonde in a light blue dress…
my first thought? Cinderella.
Yet I pirouette more like Mowgli,
junglewild and treedazzled.
Bare foot, sharded beer bottle,
painheelstumble—
the closest things I know
to perfectglassfit.
But you dreamed me.
I was a little less
with you than you wanted…

A shift—a cobalt smear of time. A study
in skywide eyes,
the taptaptap of index 'tween my shoulder blades.
Check for hollow spots inside me—
inside me sound echoes like an empty house.
I'd like to climb through
the boarded-up windows,
wrap myself in your sternummap,
your dogeared paperbacks,
curl my pinky around your Sanskrit
and make an *ahimsa* promise.

But maps are infamous for resisting
familiar folds, every new crease
a lesson in letting go. I draw
the bow of your upper lip
taut—deep breath, then release—
watch you arc across clouds
lightninglike, moonfaced, eyes
hellblue,

mouth open as if calling *ah...*
but this
is syllable unfinished.
I wait for wind to throw back the rest
of the word, a fish too small
plucked off the line,
iridescent scales flapping
blonde then blue,
dripping with midnight confusion,
believing the catching only when it sees the reflection
of the tear in its lip.

Life of the Hypotenuse

In Fort Wayne, Indiana, red and blue flashes converge, bouncing off bricks of an apartment building. They say a man's cornered inside with a shotgun. Leaving, I can tell from siren screeches the west road is blocked and I'll need another way home. I'm no stranger to detours. So, I stay out a while. Something sludgy on the harp strings of my thoughts stops them from resonating like they should. In Albuquerque, New Mexico, the other half of my bed rests under a heavier blanket; meanwhile, the distribution of sheets is all off. Something about altitude and angle makes rocks slide down the mountain; in some ways, entropy is just the gravity of time. I imagine I can smell my lover, though transmissions between organ and brain are staticky—it works if I trace my nose straight from the center of his chest hair to his belly button. But I always get lost in the digressions of his spread fingers, the parallel ribs, the parabola of his reaching tongue.

Social media reminds me of others in radius. A redhead's vantage in a rooftop photo is enough for me to plot from the bar the triangle steps by which he would lose his road. I'll never understand why so many men choose opposite over adjacent... We ought to be direct with each other, live the life of the hypotenuse, but half of us fly as the crow while fearing the other half's tangents. Who can say anyone makes it home safe anymore?

Perhaps it was all an accident. Perhaps he just forgot to carry the one. Perhaps I never asked for proof either way.

After hours of standoff, cops break the door to an empty room. That night, I roll off the vacant middle of the bed and elbow-smack the carpeted floor.

The ley lines are straight, even if our cracked slabs of sidewalk are not.

The Evolution of Gills

If I were only skin-deep,
I'd watch radioactive waves slip
past—and wonder, Would I
do any good, to turn them?
Or better they focus
like a magnifying glass
or microscope
to kill a cancer planted inside
and not you, dear one.

The secret of the gods of myth
is they made the cancer
part of themselves, damming up
veins so nothing got
back to their hearts. Of course,
when they died, aristocrats
followed, dropping powder wigs
for Isosceles smiles, calculated
to damn up men's brains
so no thought should creep
unplanned. But such bastards
to convention as we,
they could not have conceived.

Unfooled, you don a lunatic smile,
and I tuck an original voice
behind a bleary-eyed writer's cliché.
Because, I know, given the chance
I'd use my pen to assassinate—
for that's how it might feel, though
hands holding my head underwater
present a solid case for self-defense.
Instead, I develop gills: a great
blasphemy to the hands that hold heads.

You know they cannot dam you up.
But brimstone in your eye and the hard
line of your jaw threaten
you might do it yourself for spite.
But, it just isn't over yet. The wilds in you
are everything they've sought to tame.
These they cannot have unless you consent.

Improv

A bell chimes the hour
somewhere in this city of churches.
We shuffle cold under street lights.
I'd forgotten the fluorescent buzz of just *looking*
into new irises, at the curve of nose and tooth.
My stiff hands ball in shallow pockets.
Autumn came like a sledgehammer this year.
Collarbones turn up like question marks.

I forget how this scene goes,
but the first rule of improv
                    is always say yes.

I pivot on my toes, one side of a Rubik's cube, matching
black boot socks, hugs hello and goodbye, and what it might be
                to hold you just
                for Tuesday, for coffee, or
                for *see you next time.*

There's always a pause between the opening car door
and the leaving.
I never got the hang of how to use it.

I want to hear how old you were when your first pet died,
and I'll tell you how to turn over stones
                and push the hair out of my eyes.

You should know I have a past
freckled as the bridge of my nose.
I am capable of great
gestures, hair days, follies… feats of hope.
I've skinned my knees—and will again—just come on:
thumb the hollow of my cheek and
                ask me a question.

Chalk and Charcoal

I'm friends with fossils
who copy themselves year after year on carbon paper,
people of ash not sinew, not bone
but chalk and charcoal,
drifting like snowflakes
or bits of burnt paper
that disintegrate at the lightest fingertip touch.

Are you no different?
You, like dark-roast coffee
strong, an acquired taste,
you who stoke sparks and quote Chekhov
all stubble and calluses and chapped knuckles…
I followed by your heat,
my Hansel with a trail of embers.

You with your Secretariat heart
lashing against my ear through your shirt:
if loving me was like trying to clean windows
with peanut butter and a baseball bat,
loving you was like trying to floss my teeth
with an industrial-strength laser.

Unsafe Passage

Two and a half days of losing my goddamn mind to abandonment lies
of the empty womb…It's worse since the great rift, the smashed compass.
Waves splash on raft beams.

Ashore, the Crimson Queen of Hearts screams piccolo notes only dogs
should hear, waving her thyrsus of harmonics, flinging rabid drops of
sound till ears ring with her wailing.

Davy Jones' specter reels from my last hits, but I'm broken-knuckled,
too battered for dancing 'round a ring anymore. "Again!" the interrogator
demands,

but I'll snap my own neck straightaway rather than with taped-up eyelids
bear witness to the freckle on some tilted breastbone I'm sure got you off.

What about my freckles? *Too sensitive.* Too many holes drilled in psyche.
A tiny mirror taps nerve ends at the tips of my canine teeth. *Too smart for
my own good, Mom?* That's an esophageal block I can't swallow right now.

*   *   *

Round two. I smack myself around once the hand's whiskey-gloved enough.
Magnetic poles flip, and the needle spins hysterically. Sea legs lost. I light
a signal fire,

sow saltwater droplets in blanket furrows for lack of a shoulder seam,
and trade gut-punches with my shadow, who taunts that all roses are just
painted. Even yours.

When I ask for your palm it means please anchor me to this room:
star charts say I'll drift through the wall and to another dimension.

First in my class of small-town neurotics, now mad captain of this ship of
bones.

I set sail a few times and barely scuttled back alive, washing monster
gore, my own red cells, off my fingers in public sinks since I was ten.
I'm sorry

I clogged all the drains with sand. I was testing for a passage through.
Last night I woke at four in the morning, lights still on, sternum damp
from battle sweat,

In a pile of books and a little notepad with the open pen luckily not
bleeding onto the sheet in a spot where your elbow could have been.

I might've rowed away into the ink. Fuck it—I know I'm replaceable.
Exhibit A is the shadow of the Queen on the wall above Davy's reclined
form.

Exhibit B: the washaway of my tracks when I step out of the saltwater.
And Exhibit C is, I guess, whatever you're doing instead when I give up
and resign to let my gloves fall tonight.

The Space of Fingernails

I'm sorry my offering is a dead-end road,
a tree-lined lane only to a turnaround.
I need you wordlessly, my tequila heart your
thick wrist—a rope I can trust to hold
for the canyon descent,
a splint for my broken-ankle limp.
I have only the space of fingernails,
of eyelashes, between moods
changeable more than a summer storm sky.
You are a talisman to repel evil spirits,
a cairn in the desert where I am still   dust-caked, rebuilding
my *papier-mâché* Earth that he crunched.   You know that
I meant what I said about cactus roots.
So depend on my averted eye and see
I'm floating   out among planets,
tugging the gravity
                    of one
                              to slingshot
                                        free   of another.

Hide and Seek

Yesterday I called in missing
Then lay low at the movies

I dissolved into black
Like salt-tang on popcorn tongue

Ducked between arm rests
Wanting to stay unfound

Like a toy two days in the sandbox
"You know it's not so bad here

The grit will wear me smooth
New paint and I'll be anything"

I counted to 100 ten different ways
Got tired of being "It"

Always chasing
So I opted out

When one door closes
Think I'll just stay outside

"Olly Olly oxen free"
Times infinity

Flame-Lit Seeing

I looked for you in the sky but found Orion
roving among winter constellations,
with rough hunters who cannot fathom the leaves only want
a breeze's delicate caress, a simple kiss of starlight;
men whose overtures are the crunch of boots
snapping ribs, always breaking and entering through
splinters of demolished front doors.

I look for you when the raccoon rustles the brush,
around your eye the blackened rim
of the iron containment ring
requisite for true flame-lit seeing.

I examine the bark of my half-transformed ankle,
Struck that the lover I escaped could have rooted me
shuddering cold, with you at arms' reach.

I've heard trees braced for impact
hours before the detonation at Hiroshima.

Last night, though, I dreamt the bombs never fell,
that the mushroom cloud had been subsumed by your cowlick
and the predators were all turned to stars.
My twisted roots have become feet again.
If I run scared, I promise it won't be away.

Maybe I'll always remember you as the fire in your beard,
that scotch and soda mouth, the wisp of smoke from a memory told
lit up like the burning end of a cigarette
at the drawing in of breath,
that hypostatic moment when anything might be said.

The Stray

Twenty-seven years old, and still chipping nail polish on guitar strings,
barefoot in blue jeans, veins in the tender arch
        like zebra stripes
                         I loved
          when I was a child...

Twenty-seven years old, still eating leftovers of my grandparents' karma,
saving earthworms from rainy sidewalk tramplings,
always opening splintering-wood doors elders warn to leave closed.

Stopped chasing lost dogs that never learned "sit" or "stay,"
but I started to wander.
          Dunno how to belong when nobody belongs back.

Twenty-seven years old and a mouthful of cavities.
               No wonder
         I get lost   in gaps between things.

And still, grass stains on my knees, tugging out roots
for an answer to a question nobody ever asks.
I try to French braid my hair like my mom did,
but fingers keep slipping, toddlerclumsy.

No one made me feel dewy grass under my heel
or the scrapecut of gravel in my palm
like he did. Just a peek under the Band-Aid tears the scab.
And I'm filled up with splinters and storm clouds.

John

Christ said let the dead bury the dead.
Yet there you stoop,
digging with your father's wallet,
spattering your knees and thighs.
A silhouette obscured in heavy fog, still those eyes
electric blue in all this rotted forest.

If my heart is caged it's that my ribs
are petrified butterfly wings,
from a giant species gone extinct long before
you or I drew breath.
Everything is fragile
when you look with eyes that shoot laser beams.

You will see the web again, right where it was the day before
you knocked it down. You will see a man's nearly torn-
off fingertip knit back together.
Get up off your knees. Resilience, darling,
is a lie we tell into existence,
is a next meal from God knows where, is the miracle
of making our vestigial selves work again.

Cranial Warming

Her mind is sun
turning skin pink from inside—
You may not be the bride,
silly girl, don't you know
tectonic separation is the natural order?
Pangeia is an illusion.

"I now pronounce you
Island and Icecap."
(A stupid, slow icecap—
ha, isn't that *funny?*)
Her sides split
unhumorously.

"You're not handling this
with grace."
Island sneers over his cigarette.
Part of Icecap disappears
in saltwater levels rising
feeling mean, wanting a Titanic
to grind between molars
suck like a shot of vodka down
her cheeks warm with alcohol flush
and indignance.

She floats with her chin
too close to the surface to tell
whether they alone are sinking
or all oceans are rising.

You May Surrender at Any Time

These borders have been marked
their curvaceous boundaries sketched   by fingernails
on backs   freckled with ash   and blood
The truce depends on technicalities
(You may wake to sounds of spattering)

The no-fly zone extends 500 miles north of your belly button
I've studied maps   scratched branch-tip in brown earth
raised scars of razor wire
in aerial drone photos   elevation dizzying
And what is gravity but something in us
that yearns to crash   that hungers
to be brought down?

The truce depends on self-control
parenting ourselves amidst porcelain and glass
we break   we buy   so you cannot afford, you say, to look
with your hands
Then ask yourself whether the explosions you hear
are mortars
or fireworks
or shattering plates

So pull the alarm   the protocols are clear
take evasive maneuvers
disguise your heat signature

or race me for control of the skies
I can promise you   the paranoid don't survive
only the lucky

Is refusal to love another kind   of cold war?   Ask me
        point-blank   and I'll return fire   full-force

                The truce depends on Newton's third
                for every action   reaction
                    for every ton   megaton

Missing Person Report

Evidence remains
this gray hair   a blown fuse
a bruise on a cloudy sky

a sulfur smell   of spoilt eggs
when the power came back on

In my arms her baby squeaks and snuffles
and I imagine the chill that settled when the house
became the silent vacuum of space

when a drop of blood in a bowl
attracted a supernova
grief as barely formed as stem cells
black and open as the universe

She told me she saw them in dreams
those tiny hands that were not
yet hands at all

How confusing it must have been
not to say a name
she had not even
picked out

Dropouts

Love is like a test
we fall asleep and drool on.

Cold Case

I'm cross-legged among our dry, dusty artifacts,
wearing your old shirt with holes under the sleeves.

I could write a book about how your body has become smaller,
how it is somehow the most—the all?—I ever knew of you.

We were an arrhythmia in the heartbeat.
We were for a season.
We were a sick day or vacation.

I never got the memo;

I loved you then as I always still do.

Escape Velocity

This body is not an asteroid   This body is
           a collapsed stowaway
        cargo-hold-cramped en route to your town
I try to send
   a distress signal

      I say, "Love"   and mean
                something overhead

send a photo of myself sleeping and mean
            "You are sleeping"
                    Meanwhile
pulsars are flickering

  eerie deep-space lullabies in the richest black more soot-
                                stained
than my cracked knuckles
                  This hand may be
           too rough to wake you
so I don't touch

     I say nothing   now that
            freeze-dried tongue can't
                form
right galaxies
      my scanners only pick up   rumors of clouds
                    over Mars like
      the you I missed out on

            My final descending thought:
it's possible I could
      have never loved you
            enough

Before **A. C. Dreher** became a career firefighter, she taught writing and classical mythology at Indiana University-Purdue University Fort Wayne, where she earned an M.A. in English in 2014. Her poetic influences include Paul Celan and Nate Pritts. When she isn't working or writing, she may be found running, playing guitar, or exploring outer space via sci-fi video games.

www.ingramcontent.com/pod-product-compliance
Lightning Source LLC
LaVergne TN
LVHW021124080426
835510LV00021B/3311